33
Practical Tips
for
PUBLIC SPEAKING

CARMEN CORRAL

Author Carmen Corral
Translated from Spanish to English by Amber Aguilar

Copyright © 2016 Carmen Corral

All rights reserved.

ISBN-13: 978-1537544878
ISBN-10: 153754487X

Speak only when you feel your words are better than your silence.

Chinese Proverb

CONTENTS

1. Get to know your audience 11
2. Define the objective of your presentation 13
3. Get in depth with your topic 18
4. Select your ideas; you cannot talk about everything 21
5. Use a clear structure 25
6. Make an impact with your introduction 27
7. A memorable finish 30
8. Do not write your speech down 32
9. Adapt your language to your audience 35
10. Use repetition 38
11. Do not use your visual presentation as notes . 41
12. Use simple visual aid materials 43
13. Practise, practise, practise 45
14. Speak WITH your audience, not for them 47
15. Don't run, it is not a race 49
16. Use pauses and let the audience breathe 51
17. Vo-ca-lise 53
18. Emphasise key words and important phrases 55

19. Avoid fillers 57
20. Look at your audience 59
21. Move naturally 60
22. Speak with passion 62
23. Smile 63
24. Involve your audience 64
25. Prepare to improvise 67
26. Do not imitate others 68
27. Face your fear of public speaking 70
28. Picture yourself succeeding 72
29. Take a few moments to relax before your presentation 74
30. Drink water 75
31. During your presentation, do not judge yourself 76
32. Congratulate yourself on the presentation 77
33. Self-assess your speech 78

To communicate is to share. To share is an act of generosity in which we share our ideas and opinions with other people. It is a shame to stop communicating just because the group of people listening is large.

As a child, I was one of those girls who would hide behind the classmate in front of me so that the teacher would not ask me questions, and it was not because of not knowing the answers - at least not always. It was because I was embarrassed to speak in front of the whole class. I was afraid my classmates would laugh at me if I said something wrong.

As the years went on, the embarrassment and the fear of being laughed at disappeared, but the anxiety and fear of being judged when speaking in front of a group of people remained. I have attended many conferences where I have been left wanting to ask the speaker a question. And I didn't, because I was scared to speak in front of so many people. I have been left many times wanting to say many things.

Until one day I said to myself, "That is enough. I don't want to have to stay quiet – I am going to learn to speak in public". In truth, it was not so spontaneous. I was involved in a very interesting project in the company I was working for, and when it got to launching the project, my boss told me, "You are going to deliver some information sessions to the whole company." You can imagine my reaction; I broke out in a cold sweat. And at that moment, I decided: I want to learn to speak in public – if I have to do it, I want to do it well.

I started to learn techniques and resources for public speaking, and began to practise. I joined Toastmasters (if you still do not know them, they are an international not-for-profit organisation for improving communication and leadership skills) and bit by bit, as I learnt how to communicate with an audience, the fear began to turn into enjoyment. Today, public speaking is my pleasure. I no longer keep quiet the things I want to say – at least, not because of the number of listeners.

> *"To communicate is to share"*

Do not allow fear or lack of preparation to stop you sharing your ideas. Do not allow the number of listeners to determine whether or not you communicate.

This book will give you 33 practical tips for improving your communicative skills in front of an audience. It is a practical guide to public speaking, applicable in all kinds of situations where you have to speak in front of an audience: company meetings, conferences, training, social events, celebrations, and so on.

It is not simply a book of techniques to get over your fear of public speaking – although you will find some of those. Because I believe that if you learn how to communicate in front of a group of people, and you practise, experience will help you get over your fear.

> *"The way to develop self-confidence is to do the thing you fear to do and get a record of successful experiences behind you." Dale Carnegie*

The 33 practical tips are in a logical order that you can follow to prepare and deliver your presentation, although if you prefer, you can read the tips in the order you want.

You will find advice on what to say, how to say what you want to say, and how to control nerves.

1. Get to know your audience

It is easier to speak to people we know than to strangers. Sometimes, with people we don't know, we do not even know what to talk about, because we do not know what their interests are.

Before starting to prepare your presentation, you must get to know your audience. Of course, this does not mean each person individually, but the group: Who are they? How many of them are there? What do they all have in common? What are their interests? What do they like? What do you have in common with that group of people? What do they need? Why do they want to listen to you? What are they hoping to get out of your presentation?

Your speech is not about you, it is about them. They don't want to hear what interests you, they want to hear about what interests them. That is why it is so important that you know and understand them.

> *"Seek first to understand, then to be understood." Steven Covey*

If you know your audience, you can adapt your presentation to their needs and expectations. For example, delivering a customer service presentation to a group of seven doctors is not the same as delivering it to a group of one hundred lawyers. Their expectations will be different, because their clients are different, their interests are different. If you already have a presentation on the topic, you should adapt it to each occasion, bearing your audience in mind.

Also, knowing your audience will make it easier for you to speak to them confidently, because they are not strangers any more: you know now what interests them.

To know your audience, do your research. Speak to acquaintances who have the same concerns as your audience. Obtain any information possible from the person organising the event. Look online: on websites, communities and forums where people similar to your audience congregate, and find out what they are talking about. Put yourself in their shoes, forget your own interests for a moment and think as if you were a member of that group.

Understanding your audience is fundamental to enabling them to understand you and your message.

2. Define the objective of your presentation

"Begin with the end in mind." The 7 Habits of Highly Effective People, Stephen Covey

Before you start preparing the content of your presentation, it is important to define its objective. What are you hoping to achieve by its delivery? Preparing a presentation to entertain guests at a ceremony is not the same as informing people about a company's latest results.

A presentation can be categorised into one of the following 4 general objectives:

- **To entertain.** When the only aim is to entertain your audience. It can inform or inspire, but the main aim is to entertain. For example, telling a story to a group of friends, or making a toast at a family celebration. In this last example, your objective could also be to inspire. You decide what your main objective is.

- **To inform.** When you present any kind of information. Your intention is simply to inform your audience. For example, presentations on company results, or delivering training. You can include elements of persuasion or inspiration, but the principal aim is to inform.

- **To persuade.** When what you are hoping to achieve with your presentation is for your audience to take some kind of action after listening to you. For example, commercial presentations, sales pitches, political meetings, etc.

- **To inspire**. When your main objective is to make your audience think, to move them emotionally, and to bring about a change in their consciousness - for example, motivational speeches. Often, these include elements of persuasive speeches and the two can be confused. Ask yourself what your ultimate objective is – to persuade, or to inspire? The two are different. Do you want a change in your audience's conscience? Or do you want them to do what you are suggesting (examples could include buying your product or voting for your proposal)?

Always keep your presentation's main objective in mind. You can use elements of other objectives in your speech, but never lose sight of your ultimate objective.

Let me give you an example: presenting your company's marketing goals for the coming year. The main objective of the presentation can be **informing** the audience; colleagues from other departments. I will also include part of my speech for persuading the audience, so that they support and cooperate with attempting to achieve these marketing goals. If my main objective is to inform, much of the presentation will be information and data, and just a small part – requesting their cooperation - will be dedicated to persuading.

However, if my main objective is to **persuade** the audience to cooperate with me in achieving my goals, the presentation will be very different. Rather than including so much information, I will be appealing to the importance of their cooperation, the benefits to them, and so on.

Once you have defined your main objective, define your **specific objective**. To do so, you must answer the question: what are you actually hoping to achieve with your presentation?

In the example I gave, if the general objective is to inform, the specific objective could be "to present the marketing department's goals for the coming year". If we opt for a persuasive speech, the specific objective could be "to obtain the collaboration of other departments in achieving yearly marketing goals".

If we are preparing a toast for our best friend's wedding, our specific objective could be "amuse the audience with anecdotes of things that have happened to us together", while the general objective is to entertain the audience. If our objective is to inspire, the specific objective could be "to incite positive emotions about how beautiful love is". In this speech, we could also include anecdotes, but we would orientate them towards inciting this emotion.

If you have to give your presentation a title, do not use your specific objective as the title. A conference's title should pique people's curiosity and interest. The specific objective is a phrase to help you keep your objective in mind at all times. Often, it will reveal and foreshadow too much of your presentation to your audience.

Last but not least, we are going to define the **emotions** that we want to evoke in our audience (happiness, optimism, love, anger, sadness, fear, surprise, confidence...) Whether we mean to or not, our words stir up emotions for those who are listening. Even an informative speech will generate certain emotions in its listeners. For example, if we are presenting a company's results, the audience may feel confidence, optimism, surprise or anger. It depends on what we are communicating, and how.

People are emotional beings. Emotions influence what we interpret and what we remember. Do not leave to chance the emotion that your speech will incite in your audience. Begin with the end in mind. Decide what emotions you want your audience to feel when they hear your speech.

You can transmit different emotions throughout your speech. At this stage, decide what the general emotion is that you want to transmit to your audience – the emotion you want them to attach to the memory of your message.

By defining our objectives (general objective, specific objective, and emotions we want to transmit) before starting to prepare our speech, we will have something to guide us. We know where we are going – something fundamental for choosing a path.

> *-Would you tell me, please, which way I ought to go from here?*
> *-That depends a good deal on where you want to get to – answered the Cheshire Cat.*
> *-I don't much care where – said Alice.*
> *-Then it doesn't much matter which way you go – answered the Cheshire Cat.*
> *Alice in Wonderland, Lewis Carroll.*

The objectives of your speech are your destination on a journey you are guiding your audience along.

3. Get in depth with your topic

You probably have a lot of ideas about the topic you are going to be speaking about. If not, do some research: look online, ask people who might have knowledge or opinions on the subject. Even if you know the topic well, it is always a good idea to do some research. There may be new updates and you may discover new points of view and opinions. Seeing how others approach the topic and what ideas they have will be useful for you in terms of gaining a wider view when it comes to creating your speech.

Before deciding how to approach the topic, use one of the following techniques to generate and organise your ideas. These are techniques that will help you free your creativity and broaden your perspective.

- **Brainstorm**: Take a blank sheet of paper and a pen and start writing everything that springs to mind regarding the topic. The key to effective brainstorming is to write down everything, absolutely everything, that comes to mind. Do not try to decide if it is suitable or not. There will be time for choosing and discarding ideas later. Do not try to organise your ideas on the paper during the brainstorming phase. Just write them down as they come into your head, wherever your hand guides you on the paper.

- **Mind map**: To organise your brainstorm you can create a mind map. Write the topic in the centre of your sheet of paper and add your ideas, connecting them to each other and categorising them.
- **Cubing**: This consists of looking at your topic from 6 different perspectives:
    1. Describe the topic. What is it like?
    2. Compare the topic with other similar ones. How is it similar and how is it different?
    3. Associate your topic with another. What does it tell you? Be creative.
    4. Analyse the topic's parts. How are they related to each other? Are all the parts equally important?
    5. Application. What can you do with it? Is it useful? How can I use it? Who can use it??
    6. Arguments for and against your topic. What are its benefits? How might some people disagree?
- **Interview your topic**. Treat your topic as if it were a person and interview it.
    - What is your full name? Does anyone call you anything else?
    - How do the dictionary and encyclopaedia define you?
    - When were you born? What were the circumstances?

- Are you still alive? If not, how did your existence come to an end?
- What group do you belong to? Are you the same as others in your group?
- Can you be divided into parts? How?
- Were you different in the past? How?
- Will you be different in the future? How?
- Have you ever felt misunderstood?
- What is your purpose?
- What are you similar to and why?
- How are you different and why?
- Are you better than something or someone? In what way?
- Are you worse than something or someone? In what way?
- When people talk about you, what do they say?
- Are there any facts or statistics I should know about you?
- Is there someone I should talk to about you – an expert, for example?
- Is there a famous saying or quotation about you?
- Have you been in the news?
- Should I research you further?

Getting to know the topic, researching it and "subjecting" it to some of these creative techniques, will help us to know it in greater depth and from different perspectives.

4. Select your ideas; you cannot talk about everything

After having got to know your topic in depth, you now have a wider view of it and many ideas – too many ideas. We cannot talk about everything. We would overwhelm our audience with so much information. Remember not to bite off more than your audience can chew.

If we want to get our message across to the audience, and for them to remember it, we must select just three main ideas. That's right – just three.

Let's imagine I am preparing a presentation on recycling, and these are some of my ideas on the topic:

- Advantages: environment, less pollution…
- Disadvantages: cost…
- Obstacles: learning how to recycle, resistance to change, investment…
- Types of recycling
- Countries that recycle most and the results of that
- Who participates in the recycling process: people, government, corporations…

- How to recycle: paper, glass, plastic, metal, organic waste, batteries…

The main objective of my speech is to persuade, and the specific objective is "To convince my neighbours to recycle their domestic waste". My audience are my neighbours; I know them and I have analysed their interests. It is in their interests for the neighbourhood to function well, without them having to go to great effort.

I could speak about all the aforementioned points, compressing them into the time available for my presentation. It is possible, but hardly efficient. We would overwhelm the audience with such a quantity of information.

However, if we choose just three ideas, the audience will receive our message much better. And I will choose the ideas bearing in mind the audience's interests and the objective of the presentation.

In this example, we might choose the following three ideas:

1. Advantages of recycling
2. Who participates in the recycling process
3. How to recycle

To make our speech more effective, let us turn each of those ideas into a message. For example:

1. Recycling benefits us all (Advantages)
2. Recycling is up to everyone (Who)
3. Recycling is simple and anyone can do it (How)

Now, our ideas are organised and clear. We know what we want to get across. If our ideas are organised, we can transmit our message clearly, and it will be easy for the audience to understand and remember it.

We could introduce one of the points we left out, but we would do so with the aim of supporting one of the three main ideas. For example, we could talk about the countries with the highest levels of recycling in order to support our message "recycling is up to everyone".

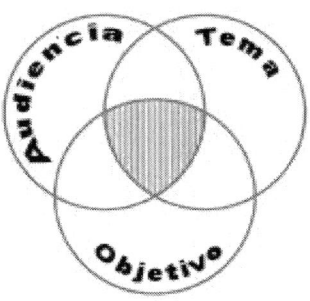

You know your audience, objectives and topic. Where the three overlap is where your speech is.

If you have to deliver a presentation but you do not have a concrete topic, choose one; start by getting to know your audience. Explore the themes you could talk about. You can brainstorm for this. Join the circle – audience and topic. If you know what your general objective is – entertain, inform, persuade, or inspire – join that circle with the audience and then with the "topic" circle.

Remember to select just three ideas, bearing in mind your audience's interests and the presentation's objective. Turn those three ideas into messages that support your main message and the specific objective of your presentation.

5. Use a clear structure

Think of your presentation as a story, because whatever your objective or your audience, it is a story you are going to tell – and as such, it should have a beginning, middle and end.

As a rule of thumb for any type of speech, these are the time frames you should use for each of those parts:

- Introduction – 5-10% of your time
- Development – 80-90%
- Conclusion – 5-10%

These time frames are a guide only – in some cases, it may be necessary to increase or decrease them depending on what is needed for your speech.

Your speech may fit the universal structure used for telling stories:

- There was once a _____
- Every day, _____
- Until one day _____
- Then, _____
- Until finally _____

This structure is very popular in fiction and animation – for example, all Pixar films and shorts. And it works very well, even for more formal speeches. Many TED Talks follow this structure.

There was once a company called "my company". **Every day** (month), it invested a lot of money in marketing. **Until one day** it decided not to invest in marketing any more. **Then,** its sales decreased considerably. **Until finally** it found our marketing services and increased its sales a lot, and with lower costs.

This structure can be useful either for your whole presentation or for telling stories within the presentation.

6. Make an impact with your introduction

The introduction is the most important part. If it captures your audience's attention, you have done well already. However, if you do not manage to get their interest from the start, it will be harder for you to get it later on.

> *"You never get a second chance to make a good first impression"* Groucho Marx

Grab them with the first thing you say. First impressions count for a lot. To make sure it comes out perfectly, learn your introduction by heart. It should last between 5 and 10 per cent of your presentation's length. If your presentation is 15 minutes long, the introduction should not last longer than a minute and a half – if your presentation lasts an hour, it should be between 3 and 6 minutes.

Your introduction should pique the audience's curiosity and make them want to keep listening. To achieve this, you can use various resources:

- A story or anecdote related to the topic. If it is a personal story that has happened to you, even better. Audiences like to know things about us.
- Begin with a quotation from a famous author.

- Begin with a blunt, direct statement about your topic. For example, you could start a presentation about the environment with a sentence like: If no one charged their phone for one day, 15,000,000 kilograms of greenhouse gases could be avoided.

- Formulate a rhetorical question. (You will find more about questions in practical tip number 24: Involve your audience)

- Refer to the event you are at. If you are speaking at a ceremony, mention it. If it is a special day or something special has happened, refer to that. This will help you connect with the audience.

If the objective of your speech is to inform, the introduction should include the points you will cover during your presentation. Give a preview of the topics you will speak about. But don't give your audience all the information at this stage. If you do, they will lose interest in listening to you because they will have already heard everything that is important. Give them the most fundamental parts to pique their curiosity and to follow the structure of your presentation, just the basis of the topics you will be speaking about.

If, on the other hand, the objective of your presentation is to inspire, do not foreshadow the topics you are going to talk about. Do not present the audience with the structure of your speech during your introduction. The same applies if your speech is to entertain. Surprise is fundamental for these types of speeches.

If your speech is persuasive, you may decide to reveal your presentation's structure at the beginning, or you may not. Answering these questions will help you to assess this choice:

- Do the audience need to know the structure of my speech in order for it to be effective?
- Does the type of audience I am speaking to like to know the structure?
- Will my presentation be difficult to follow if I do not present the structure at the beginning?
- Is the element of surprise unimportant in my presentation?

If the answer to most of these questions is yes, introduce the basis of your presentation.

Learn your introduction by heart. You might decide not to write your speech word for word and to leave some room for improvisation in parts of your presentation, but never do this in your introduction. Remember how important it is to capture your audience's attention. Anyway, a good introduction will give us confidence in ourselves.

7. A memorable finish

It is well-known that what we remember best is what we heard last. Do not finish with "That's all" or "I have nothing else to say". You do not want that to be how they remember your message.

If the introduction was important for preparing the audience to listen, the conclusion is equally important because it is what your audience are going to take away from your message.

As with your introduction, you should memorise your conclusion.

To open your conclusion, you can use phrases like: "in conclusion", "I would like to finish by saying", "To sum up"…

Your conclusion should have a positive impact on your audience. To achieve this, you can use various resources:

- Quotation from a famous person.
- A story or anecdote related to the topic, though this should be short and simple.
- Rhetorical question: Do you want to keep seeing the same results?
- Refer back to the start of your presentation. This type of ending is very effective as it

closes the circle of your presentation, and that is appealing to an audience. It can also refer to some story or idea that you mentioned during the presentation. For example, if you told a story about your grandfather, you can finish by saying "As my grandfather said...", or "My grandfather was right..."

- Call to action. This type of ending is ideal if your speech is persuasive. Tell your audience what you want them to do after having listened to you, and what's in it for them.

Your conclusion should transmit and reinforce the message of your presentation.

Want them to remember your message?

"Things end but memories last forever"

Give your audience a reason to remember your presentation.

8. Do not write your speech down

Speaking is different from writing. Writing a speech is very different from writing an article, story or email. We do not use the same resources when we speak as when we write. For that reason, when you are writing a speech, you must bear in mind that it is not being written to be read. There are experts dedicated to doing just that, but our objective is not to be one of those experts – at least, not in this book. Our objective is to speak, not to write.

If we write our speech word for word and present it just like that, our presentation will probably not sound natural. Even if we know the content by heart and do not need to read it, these tend to be artificial-sounding speeches.

So, how do I remember my speech if I cannot write it down? We *are* going to write it, but to be heard, not read. There are two techniques:

- Define the ideas you will talk about. Organise them. Write an outline of them. Write the introduction and the conclusion. Now, start to present the topic out loud. You can record yourself or take note of the important phrases you are saying as you speak. Even if you have already written your introduction and conclusion, check how those words sound when you pronounce them.

- The other technique consists of writing your speech from start to finish. But do not become too enamoured yet of the eloquence of your words and phrases, because the next step is to unwrite them. Start to rehearse out loud, being very flexible with everything you have written, in order to modify it. Let yourself insert new words and phrases, change the ones you have for others more appropriate to spoken language. As with the previous technique, you can record yourself or take notes as you go along.

The difference between these two techniques the basis we are developing our speech from – just with an outline, or with the text. Depending on the person or topic, one technique will be easier than the other. As you can see, the only difference is in how we begin preparing our speech. After that, the two techniques develop in the same way: speaking out loud, rehearsing and writing or rewriting our speech.

During the adaptation of our speech to spoken language, some people will find it necessary to write the whole speech word by word – for others, writing the key phrases will suffice.

Bear in mind one basic principle of the differences between spoken and written language.

In writing, as a general rule, repetitions are not allowed. A text is incorrect if it contains constant repetitions. However, spoken language uses the repetition of basic concepts, words, and important phrases as a resource to help the audience remember.

When we read, we do it at our own pace. We are looking at it and we can re-read whatever we want. But when we listen, we must adapt to the pace of the speaker. If he/she presents an idea and then quickly moves on to another, we will very likely get lost. When we speak, we need to give the audience time to digest what we are saying – that is why we should present an idea and repeat it using other words, to enable the audience to understand, to explain it in details and to close that idea by presenting it again.

In spoken language we use shorter sentences, for the same reason – to make it easier to understand.

You are going to speak in public, you are not writing for the public. So prepare your speech by speaking, not writing.

9. Adapt your language to your audience

I am sure that you have been to at least one conference where you have become lost during the presentation because the speaker is using language that is too technical. And you look around you and realise you are not the only one who does not understand; the rest of the audience is as lost as you are.

The opposite can also happen: what the speaker is presenting can be too basic for the audience.

It is worth repeating how important it is to know your audience in order to deliver a successful speech. Your presentation is for the audience, not for you. You should bear in mind their interest in and prior knowledge of the topic.

Presenting a marketing plan to your colleagues in marketing is not the same as presenting it to the rest of your colleagues in other departments. Your workmates in marketing know the terminology used in marketing. People who do not work in that field will not know certain words that are very common for you. It is another thing again to deliver that marketing presentation to people outside the company, because there is terminology specific to each company. Watch out for those terms that are usual for you because you use them in your everyday work, because people from outside of your environment have no reason to be familiar with that same terminology.

If you find it difficult to speak to an audience that does not have the same knowledge as you, of course it is not a simple task; imagine how you would explain it to your grandmother in a way that she could understand.

> *"You do not really understand something unless you can explain it to your grandmother" Albert Einstein*

As well as the language you use, it is also important to consider how in-depth you go with the topic, and how you explain the concepts. Explaining how learning processes work to a group of university students in their first year, is not the same as explaining it to professors. For students hearing a speech on the topic for the first time, you should focus on the basics. However for professors, who know a lot about the topic, you should go into greater depth and tell them something that they do not already know.

Bear in mind your audience's interests too. For

example, if you are delivering a speech on how a new IT tool for accounting works to a group of IT technicians, they will be interested in the technical side of things. However, if you are explaining it to a group of accountants, they will be interested in the tool's functional side.

What if the audience is varied? If they have different levels of knowledge and interest, is it possible to meet everyone's expectations? Yes, it is. Just look at some animated films, liked as much by adults as by children. The audiences are very different – children's knowledge and interests are nothing like adults', yet there are films enjoyed by both audiences. Your speech should include resources that consider each type of audience, so that they can identify with it and see that it is at their level.

10. Use repetition

Everyone remembers Obama's famous "Yes, we can." Two of the most famous and most studied phrases in the history of public speaking make use of repetition; Obama's speech, and Martin Luther King's "I have a dream".

I have a dream - **Martin Luther King (1963)**

I have a dream that one day this nation will rise up and live out the true meaning of its creed: "We hold these truths to be self-evident: that all men are created equal."

I have a dream that one day on the red hills of Georgia the sons of former slaves and the sons of former slave owners will be able to sit down together at the table of brotherhood.

I have a dream that one day even the state of Mississippi, a state sweltering with the heat of injustice, sweltering with the heat of oppression, will be transformed into an oasis of freedom and justice.

I have a dream that my four little children will one day live in a nation where they will not be judged by the color of their skin but by the content of their character.

I have a dream today.

Yes, we can - Obama (2008)

When I hear that we'll never overcome the racial divide in our politics, I think about that Republican woman who used to work for Strom Thurmond, who is now devoted to educating inner city-children and who went out into the streets of South Carolina and knocked on doors for this campaign. Don't tell me we can't change.

Yes, we can. Yes, we can change.

Yes, we can heal this nation.

Yes, we can seize our future.

… … …

Yes. We. Can.

This resource is called anaphora. It consists of repeating one word or one phrase. It brings sonority and rhythm to a speech. And what is more, it sticks in people's minds.

Do not be afraid to repeat important messages; it is

permitted in spoken language, and it is highly recommended for helping the audience to remember a speech. Give your audience a chance at remembering your speech by repeating what you consider most important.

> *"If you have an important point to make, don't try to be subtle or clever. Use a pile driver. Hit the point once. Then come back and hit it again. Then hit it a third time - a tremendous whack"* Winston Churchill

11. Do not use your visual presentation as notes

If your presentation is supported with the use of PowerPoint, Prezzi, or similar, do not create your slides as if they were your notes. The temptation to create a visual presentation as an outline to help guide us during our presentation is great, with the excuse that it will also help to guide our audience. But nothing could be further from the truth. Instead of guiding our audience, it disorientates them, as they do not know whether to pay attention to the slides or to our speech – whether to read or listen.

Do not confuse your visual presentation with your presentation:

- Never begin preparation for your presentation by creating the slides (PowerPoint).
- Your visual presentation is an *aid,* it is not your presentation. Your presentation is the sum total of everything you deliver: content, visuals, speech, and so on.
- The slides are there to support your message, not the other way round.
- Your audience should follow you, not your visual presentation.

Write your notes on a sheet, for your eyes only, with all the information you need.

12. Use simple visual aid materials

Use pictures and key words to make your visual material support your presentation. The simpler they are, the more impact they will have. Avoid using long definitions or texts. If necessary, hand out a document or report at the end that contains more detailed information and data from the presentation, in writing.

Remember: A picture is worth a thousand words.

Do not overload your slides. Ideally, use one idea per slide. Never use more than three.

If you use a whiteboard or flip chart to write on, write only your key words, and do not spend too much time writing or your audience will lose interest. Your presentation will lose its rhythm and become slow.

Try not to turn your back on the audience as you write – turn side on, so that they can still see your face. Do not speak while you are not facing the audience, as they will find it hard to follow.

Prepare all the material and resources that you will need beforehand: projector, computer, whiteboard, props, and so on.

Bear in mind that audiovisual resources can go

wrong. Do not depend on them too much – do not let your presentation be ruined by technical problems. Prepare a Plan B in case your materials let you down. Think about what you would do if you did not have visual aids at your disposal. What slides are absolutely necessary? Which could you manage without? For example, if your presentation requires a graph, and the projector or computer fails, as a last resort you could draw a rough version on a whiteboard, or for a small audience, show them a print-out of the graph. Do not overuse this emergency resource to rescue all of your slides – only do it with the fundamental ones, to prevent your presentation from becoming slow and tedious.

Choose suitable visual materials to support your message, and present it simply.

13. Practise, practise, practise

Never think that great orators do not practise. Did you think they were born with the gift of the gab and the skill of public speaking, and that just by stepping out in front of an audience and opening their mouth, their success is guaranteed?

Do you think a play can be successful without rehearsals? Or that a stand-up comedian can make his audience laugh without having practised beforehand? If not, then why should we not also rehearse any other public presentation?

Up until now, you have only prepared your presentation's content. The way you present it is just as important. And in order to prepare your presentation, you must practise it.

You can do this in front of a mirror, in front of a camera, with friends or simply by yourself. But rehearse and practise. And practise again. Practice is important for:

- Hearing ourselves and adapting our tone and vocal variety according to our message's needs.
- Adapting our body language to our message.

- Changing things that we only realise do not work when we say them out loud, as we do not write the same way we speak.
- Gaining self-confidence.

You should spend more time rehearsing than you did preparing the message. *How* is more important than *What*. If the content of your speech is not very powerful, the way you deliver it can imbue it with enough strength to turn it into a good speech. However, if your content is very good but you present it with insufficient confidence and energy, it will lose all credibility. A poor presentation can ruin a powerful message.

"90% of success is showing up" Woody Allen

14. Speak WITH your audience, not for them

We tend to view a presentation as an act or a performance. But it is not one. It is a conversation. We are going to have a conversation WITH our audience. It may be that most of the time, we are speaking, and other people involved only speak for a short space of time. However, that does not mean it stops being a conversation.

Seeing it as a conversation helps to reduce the anxiety produced by a performance. We are good at having conversations. Over the course of the day, it is what we do most. We communicate with others at work, in our families, with friends... Conversations do not make us nervous. We possess many communicative skills acquired through this experience.

If we maintain a conversation with our audience, they will perceive us to be closer to them, and our message will get across better. To do this, use conversational language. Use the language you would use if you were speaking one on one with a member of the audience.

Wherever possible, use collective pronouns and words that include you as part of the group you are speaking to. For example, "We are responsible for the environment", rather than "Humanity is responsible for the environment".

Do not worry about maintaining your authority; you will not gain authority over the subject by keeping your distance from the audience. On the contrary, closeness will give you authority because you will earn credibility. They will perceive you as an involved and interested party, who knows the topic in depth and who can help them, because you are not so different from them.

15. Don't run, it is not a race

The speed at which we speak is very important to our presentation. If we speak very quickly, we will tend not to vocalise, and we will not be clearly understood. Also, it will place our audience under stress. If we speak too fast, the audience listening will be caught up in the agitated rhythm we are transmitting.

But extremes are never good; speaking too slowly will bore our audience.

Film yourself delivering the presentation in order to determine how quickly you tend to speak. Most people usually accelerate their speech in front of an audience.

Often, we are incapable of objectively telling the speed at which we are speaking during the presentation itself. We tend to feel that we are speaking at an appropriate speed, but later we watch ourselves on video and realise that it was quite fast or quite slow. Finding out what your tendency is beforehand will help you to be aware of your pace during the presentation, and you will be able to modify it.

We each have our own natural speed of talking that we habitually use in our everyday lives - with family, at work, with friends, and so on, in small circles where we already feel comfortable. It is not a question of radically changing your natural speed, except in very extreme cases. If your speed in small circles is very slow or fast, you will need to adapt it for a larger audience, so that everyone can follow what you are saying.

Playing around with speed during the presentation will help us give it more rhythm, as well as emphasis and emotion. Speak more slowly or quickly depending on the content you are transmitting, in order to make your message more effective. Remember that a slow pace relaxes and calms the listener and helps them retain all the words in a sentence. When you speak quickly, you transmit action, agitation, euphoria. If you combine the speeds effectively, along with your intonation, this will help your presentation greatly.

16. Use pauses and let the audience breathe

Breathing is one of the most vital things we do for survival. It is something that we do without having to think about it. It seems obvious and simple. However, when we are speaking in public, we do have to remember it.

Do not speak until you run out of air. You will exhaust both yourself and your audience. Breathe and let your audience breathe.

A presentation with no pauses generates stress, anxiety and unease in the audience. It is the equivalent of reading a text with no punctuation. Try reading the following text:

> *Poor Anastasio led a lamentable existence with neither stimulus nor reason to live and he would have committed suicide a hundred times if not for the dark hope he guarded against a continued disappointment that he might too one day be visited by Love and he travelled searching for it in case when he least expected it it accosted him suddenly at a crossroads on his journey he neither coveted money since he had at his disposal a modest but for him more than sufficient fortune nor did he aspire to glory or honour or control or*

power none of the motives that drive men to try seemed to him worthy of trying for and nor could he find the slightest relief from his mortal tedium in science or art or public action.

Adapted extract (with punctuation removed) from "El amor que asalta" by Miguel de Unamuno.

Take a short pause at the end of each sentence, and breathe. Take a longer pause every time you finish an idea and move on to a different idea, in order to mark these transitions.

> *"No word was ever as effective as a rightly timed pause" Mark Twain*

Use pauses to:

- Give emphasis.
- Allow the audience to think or to retain what you have just said.

Silence is a very powerful resource.

17. Vo-ca-lise

Vocalising is not about how quickly or slowly you speak, but rather about how you pronounce the syllables. Whatever your accent is, however unaccustomed your audience is to hearing it - if you vocalise well, they will understand you.

Carry out the following exercise in order to train your vocalisation, and again before your presentation. It will warm up your voice and help you to vocalise better. Take a pen and put it in your mouth horizontally, crossing it and holding it in place with your teeth. Start to speak, as clearly as you can, without letting go of the pen. Do this exercise for a few minutes. Listen to how you speak when you remove the pen from your mouth - you will realise that you are vocalising much better.

Even if you think your vocalisation is good, it can always get better. You will get your message across much more clearly.

18. Emphasise key words and important phrases

Emphasising important words and phrases in our speech will help with two things:

- Letting the audience know what is important - that we are talking about a key idea.
- Avoiding monotony in our speech.

How can we emphasise words and phrases?

The key is to change the way we are speaking, in any way possible: if we are speaking quickly, to slow down; if we are speaking slowly, to speed up; if we are speaking loudly, to go quiet; if we are speaking quietly, to get louder...

We can use this technique for one word within a sentence, or for an entire sentence.

Decide which are the key words and phrases of your speech. You will emphasise some words differently from others; the meaning you give them will be different. For example, in the following sentence:

The good results achieved by our company over the course of last year are due to our efforts to be more original than the competition.

You can emphasis key words or parts of the sentence.

What do you want to give importance to? The good results? What you did to achieve them? Corporate spirit?

The GOOD RESULTS achieved by our company over the course of last year are due to our efforts to be more original than the competition.

The good results achieved by OUR COMPANY over the course of last year are due to our efforts to be more original than the competition.

The good results achieved by our company over the course of last year are due to OUR EFFORTS to be more original than the competition.

The good results achieved by our company over the course of last year are due to our efforts to BE MORE ORIGINAL than the competition.

THE GOOD RESULTS ACHIEVED BY OUR COMPANY over the course of last year are due to our efforts to be more original than the competition.

The good results achieved by our company over the course of last year ARE DUE TO OUR EFFORTS TO BE MORE ORIGINAL THAN THE COMPETITION.

The whole sentence could be emphasised as an important sentence within the speech.

19. Avoid fillers

Fillers are words or sounds we use while speaking that bring nothing to our speech: um, ah, and so on. Not only do they add nothing to the speech - they take away from it.

"If you, um, want different results, well, don't do, you know, the same things, right?" The fillers added to this convincing phrase of Einstein's ("If you want different results, don't do the same things") distract the listener's attention and it loses all potency.

Sometimes we use fillers out of habit - they are like a tic and are present in almost all of our communications. To eliminate them, you must first recognise them and note when you are using them. Ask a trusted person for help identifying what fillers you use.

Other times they come up because of a lack of confidence or to give us time to think about what to say next - in these cases, substitute a pause.

These are some of the fillers that need to disappear from our speech:

- Words you constantly repeat to begin, end, or change ideas. For example: So…
- Sounds between words: Um, ah, mmm

- Sounds that lengthen words and word repetition that does not bring anything to the speech: "Weeell" "and, and"

20. Look at your audience

While you are delivering your presentation, it is important that you maintain eye contact with your audience - this will help you connect with them.

If you need to use your notes, never hold them in front of your face; look at them for as little time as possible or alternate between looking at your notes and your spectators. If you use visual aids, try not to look at your material; keep looking at your audience to keep their attention on your words.

Try to look evenly around the audience - do not forget those in the back or at the front, or those to the left or right. If your audience is small, look at each person in turn at some point. Do not look at the same spot for more than twenty seconds.

Avoid looking at the ceiling or floor, or fixing your gaze anywhere where there is no one there. Avoid turning your back on your audience, and above all avoid speaking if you have turned your back; they will not hear you clearly.

21. Move naturally

Body language is just as important as verbal language. We send messages with our bodies, even without realising it. For our speech to be credible, our verbal and non-verbal language should be aligned.

When we communicate in our immediate environment, we move naturally. Naturalness comes with practice. As you are rehearsing your speech, look at your body language and modify it so that it supports your message. Practice and repetition will turn your forced gestures into natural ones.

Begin your presentation in a relaxed position that shows confidence. This will help you to transmit confidence to the audience, but will also help you to feel more confident. Stand in the centre, with both feet firmly on the floor, slightly separated and open. Your torso's centre of gravity should be in the middle. Hold your arms loose and relaxed at either side of you. You can move your hands to support what you are saying. Practise this posture and you will see that very soon it becomes a natural posture for you.

If we pace aimlessly from side to side while speaking, we will distract our audience. If you are one of those people who moves around constantly while on the phone, bear this advice in mind. Move around the space available to you, but do not do it constantly. Move, for example towards the audience, then stand in that spot for a while, adopting the aforementioned posture. Move somewhere else on the stage, then stand in that spot for a while, again adopting the posture, and so on.

You should avoid:

- Crossing your arms or hands
- Putting your hands in your pockets
- Moving your hands too much
- Pace from side to side aimlessly and agitatedly
- Turning your back on the audience
- Fiddling with objects such as pens

Practise, practise, and practise, and you will achieve naturalness.

22. Speak with passion

If you want your audience to be inspired, speak with passion. To show your passion:

- Express your emotions.
- Use adjectives: extraordinary, very, incredible…
- Consider your tone of voice - if the topic inspires you, it will transmit that enthusiasm.

What if the topic does not inspire you, but you have to speak about it anyway? It is possible, for example, that speaking about new legislation is not the most exciting topic in the world. And maybe neither you nor your audience find it very appealing. In this case, you face an important challenge. Find something interesting about the topic you have to speak about. All topics have something interesting about them. Nothing is black and white - there are a lot of shades of grey. A practical application of the topic may be interesting.

By speaking with passion, you will connect with the audience and transmit emotions.

23. Smile

Unless you are speaking at a funeral, smile. Our smile is the most powerful tool we have for empathising with the audience. We feel much closer to people who are smiling than to serious-looking people. Even if the topic is serious, there is no reason not to smile. It is a question of smiling enthusiastically, out of passion for what we are speaking about.

But your smile should be natural, not forced. When we are nervous, our facial muscles tend to tense up and our expressions can look forced and unnatural. For our smile to be authentic and natural even if we are nervous, we have to practise and warm up beforehand.

When you practise your speech, do it with a smile. There is no need to be serious while you are practising. Give yourself a smile. Practise with a smile on your lips and the smile will become more and more natural.

Before your presentation, relax the muscles of your body and especially your face. To do so, make forced facial expressions, opening and closing your mouth exaggeratedly, making faces - the more absurd and extreme they are, the more muscles you will be moving and relaxing. Massage your muscles using your fingers. You are now ready to offer a sincere, passionate and enthusiastic smile.

24. Involve your audience

Involving your audience and making them part of your presentation will help you to get their attention and let your message make more of an impression.

The most widely-used resource for this is asking questions.

You can use rhetorical questions. These are questions asked without the speaker expecting an answer, with the aim of reinforcing or reasserting his or her own point of view, assuming that the listener agrees. For example: Can we sit back and do nothing in this situation?

Instead of giving information directly, ask a question. You will generate curiosity; the audience will feel the need to know the answer. For example: How many years does it take for a Christmas tree to grow? Once the question has been asked, we want to know the answer. We do not like unanswered questions. Finding out the answer will have a greater impact than offering the information without asking the question first. A Christmas tree takes between seven and ten years to grow.

If you want even more participation, ask questions the audience can answer. Who here has a pet? Ask them to put their hands up, or show them by putting yours up. Use this resource to help the audience feel like part of the presentation. They will feel part of a group. Also, they will know that you are going to speak about something that interests them, to resolve a problem or situation.

As with all your resources, use questions in moderation. Do not overuse them. If you do, it will lose all effect and your presentation will become monotonous.

Ask the audience to do things. Depending on the conditions of the place, audience and topic, you can use this resource in different ways. For example, if you are giving a class on art history to a group of thirty students, in a classroom with tables and chairs, you could ask them to analyse a work of art in pairs. If you are giving a conference for a hundred people about public speaking, while you are showing exercises for warming up the voice, you could ask the audience to do them with you. This technique is very useful to stop your audience from "falling asleep".

Another technique you can use to involve the audience is asking volunteers to help you carry out a demonstration. Ask for volunteers and encourage participation. Try to avoid choosing a member of the audience yourself. If you do, try to choose someone who has no problem presenting themselves to the audience you are speaking to. If the person you choose has a hard time in front of the audience, they will empathise with them and have a hard time too.

Keeping your audience active will help at times when it is difficult to keep people's attention; for example, after eating.

25. Prepare to improvise

> *"I have spent all night preparing for tomorrow's improvisation"* Winston Churchill

Prepare to improvise. Yes, improvisation needs planning and practice too. You may have to improvise in presentations where the audience participate throughout, or where they can ask questions at the end of the conference. You can prepare for this. Think about the possible questions that may come up; write a list of common questions and their answers. And if someone asks you a question which is not on your list, do not worry; if you know the topic well and if you have prepared your presentation well then you will know how to respond. If not - because we are human and we do not know everything - you can respond honestly by saying that at the moment you do not have that information, and you can even commit to finding it out for the person later on.

> *"Improvisations are better when they are prepared"* Shakespeare

If you have prepared your presentation carefully then you will know how to deal with unexpected moments, because you will have confidence in your presentation.

26. Do not imitate others

Attend conferences, listen to other speakers and TED Talks, learn from the best - but do not imitate them. Why not, if they are the best? Because we each have our own style. If you imitate others, you run the risk of not appearing natural to your audience, because you are not being yourself. Audiences appreciate authentic people who present themselves in a natural way. Copying others will not help you to find your own style.

Learn the techniques used by speakers you like, and adapt them to your style.

To find your own style, you should assess what your strengths are. We all have strong points we use when speaking in front of an audience. If you do not know what they are because you have never spoken in front of a group of people, think about how you communicate with others in your personal or professional life. Those people are an audience too. All of us - yes, all of us - have acquired strengths and skills for effective communication. After all, we do not live isolated from the world; we are communicating with other humans almost all of our times, so we already know a bit about communication.

Your strengths and strong points are not things you

do perfectly; there is always room for improvement. Your strengths are things that stand out when you communicate. For example, vocal variety, tone, volume, expressiveness, body language, presenting ideas in an organised way, and so on. Analyse which things you do well. You could ask someone close to you what they consider to be your strong points when you communicate with others. Analyse which things you could improve, too.

We are used to focusing on improving our weaker points. We should do that - learn new techniques and pay attention to improving our weak points. But let us not lose sight of our strengths. We should make our strong points even better. They are things we are already good at - let us give them even more strength. For example, if one of your strengths is body language, work towards improving your movements even more - the way they accompany your message, how to move to emphasise what you are saying, and so on.

We will find it easy to improve on our strengths and win our audience over with them, because we are not starting from scratch but from an already good level. There, we will find our style.

We cannot be perfect, but we can be better.

27. Face your fear of public speaking

Fear of public speaking is the most common fear. Statistics tell us that we are more scared of public speaking than we are of death. As the American comedian Jerry Seinfeld says, "This means to the average person, if you go to a funeral, you're better off in the casket than doing the eulogy." Crazy, right?

Fear of public speaking is mostly due to multiple factors:

- fear of the unknown, of something we have never done
- fear of being rated and judged by others
- fear of messing up in front of people
- fear of being exposed
- lack of experience and practice
- fear of looking ridiculous

The good news is that this fear can be alleviated, reduced, and you can even learn to enjoy speaking in public. Yes, you can enjoy speaking in public! Many people enjoy it and anyone can turn this activity - which at first seems uncomfortable - into a pleasurable one. Do you enjoy chatting with your friends? The same way you like talking to them, why not in front of a wider group? Because we all like to be listened to.

> *"Courage is not the absence of fear, but the ability to face it"* John Putnam

In most cases, the fear of public speaking is an irrational one: "I am scared of my mind going blank". How many times has that happened to you? How many people do you know that that has happened to? And if it did happen, what is the worst that could happen? I will tell you what would happen if your mind went blank: your audience would sympathise with you, and they would understand that it is natural because it could happen to them too in your situation.

There are techniques we can apply to reduce our anxiety and nerves.

> *"It is not because things are difficult that we do not dare, it is because we do not dare that they are difficult"* Seneca

28. Picture yourself succeeding

If the mere thought of having to deliver a presentation in front of other people makes you anxious, this technique will help you. It consists of picturing yourself successfully speaking in public. You should carry out the technique some days before your presentation. Each day, take a few moments to visualise yourself speaking in front of your audience.

Find a comfortable place where you can sit or lie down. Playing relaxing music may help you. Close your eyes and relax. Take a few seconds to feel your muscles relaxing throughout your body. Take deep breaths: breathe in, hold it in your lungs for a few seconds, and exhale slowly. Imagine yourself in a place that relaxes and calms you. It can be real or imagined. Take in your surroundings: colours, scents, sounds...and think about how that environment makes you feel. Stay there until you have taken in everything around you. Bit by bit, from far away, start to visualise the place where you are going to deliver your presentation. You are still in that peaceful and relaxing place, and gradually you are moving towards the place of your presentation. Start to take it in, from your state of relaxation and tranquillity. Imagine yourself on the stage or wherever you will be speaking. For a few minutes, let your mind roam around the room; connect with your audience and picture yourself speaking passionately and energetically to your audience. Imagine their attentive faces and their applause at the end. If at any point you experience any negative thought about your presentation, discard it, eliminate it and substitute it for something pleasant.

Picturing ourselves succeeding is a very effective technique and it is widely used in different fields - for example, by great athletes. You can use this technique not just for public speaking, but for any other situation where you want to succeed.

Doing this visualisation exercise for a few days before your presentation will help you to relax and change your feelings towards it.

We will feel calmer and more relaxed because our mind will perceive the situation as familiar. It is not something new to us, because we have already imagined it.

29. Take a few moments to relax before your presentation

Before your presentation starts, do some breathing exercises. Breathe deeply a few times, from your abdomen. Inhale through your nose until your stomach puffs out, hold it for a few seconds, and exhale slowly through your mouth. This exercise calms your brain and will also help your voice to project more clearly and calmly.

Even just before starting your presentation, while in front of the audience, before you start speaking, you can take a deep breath. You will release your tension and the audience's. Your audience will connect with you, with your breathing. Your voice will sound stronger and more confident.

30. Drink water

Before your presentation, drink water. This is for two main reasons:

- **To hydrate yourself**; for your voice to be clear, you need to moisten your throat. As well as drinking beforehand, you should always have a glass of water to hand - as you speak, you may find your throat drying up and you may need to drink some more water.
- **When we drink, it calms us.** We get nervous because our brain perceives us to be in danger. In a truly dangerous situation, we do not stop to drink water. This means that drinking water when we are nervous sends a message to our brains that we are not facing any danger.

However, do not drink large amounts, or you may have to interrupt your presentation unexpectedly. Adjust the quantity according to your needs.

31. During your presentation, do not judge yourself

"Self-trust is the first secret of success"
Ralph W. Emerson

During your presentation, do not judge yourself on what you have said or not said or what you have done. Self-assessment during the presentation will not help you to continue with energy. We tend to fixate on the aspects we consider more negative and punish ourselves for them - this causes us to become more nervous still and to lose trust in ourselves.

Leave your self-assessment for the end, when you have finished. Then, you will be able to see with greater perspective, evaluating all of your presentation as a whole and in a more objective way. During the presentation, focus on your topic and your audience.

Never say that you are nervous - most of the time, even when we think we are coming across as nervous, the audience do not pick up on it. If we comment on it, all that will happen is that the audience's attention will be directed towards noticing the signs of our nervousness. Anyway, saying that we are nervous does not make us feel any less so.

32. Congratulate yourself on the presentation

Congratulations!

When you have finished speaking, the first thing you should do is congratulate yourself on having delivered the presentation.

Do this without excuses, with "if only I had...", "I should have...", or "I could have done better". We can always do better, there is always room for improvement.

Before analysing our presentation and seeing what things we can improve next time we speak in public, congratulate yourself - because what you have done is important, and it is a necessary step in your learning process. When we learn to ride a bike, every time we get on we are practising and every practice is more important to keep improving our technique. It is the same with public speaking. Every time we do it, we are practising and improving our technique.

One more time: Congratulations!

33. Self-assess your speech

After you have congratulated yourself, it is time to analyse how your presentation went.

Start by going over everything you did well. Then analyse which things you would like to do differently next time. Evaluate what you have learned too, and how you felt during the presentation.

Download your self-assessment guide free from the following website:

www.bit.ly/speechassess

If there was anyone you know in the audience, you can ask them what they thought of your presentation. That way, you will hear the point of view of a member of the audience.

If you have to deliver the same presentation again, self-assessment is very important in order to improve your speech. If you are not going to speak about the same thing again, self-assessment is important as a learning process for later occasions where you have to speak in public.

Knowing your strong points and areas for improvement is the starting point for progressing and improving your communication skills. Do not forget your strong points, they are your strengths; you already have those qualities and you can always profit from them further.

The most important tip of all: **dare to communicate** - with experience comes confidence. Seize every opportunity to practise. You can start with small, trusted groups, family or friends, or in an environment as small as you facing a camera.

Try these 33 tips and other techniques and resources you know of. Adapt them to your needs, take what works for you, and find your own style.

Communicate and share your ideas with the world.

Do you have any question or any comment? Feel free to send an email to the author Carmen Corral: carmencorral@objetivocoaching.com

Do you want to continue improving your public speaking skill? Carmen Corral offers public speaking coaching. Book a first 20 minutes session for free to learn more. info@objetivocoaching.com

More than 33 TIPS

Receive more free tips for PUBLIC SPEAKING on your email

Subscribe at
www.bit.ly/publicspeaking33

Made in the USA
Middletown, DE
05 September 2017